IMAGES
of America

SANDERS CONFECTIONERY

IMAGES
of America

SANDERS CONFECTIONERY

Greg Tasker

ARCADIA
PUBLISHING

Published by Arcadia Publishing
Charleston SC, Chicago IL, Portsmouth NH, San Francisco CA

Printed in the United States of America

Library of Congress Catalog Card Number: 2005939030

For all general information contact Arcadia Publishing at:
Telephone 843-853-2070
Fax 843-853-0044
E-mail sales@arcadiapublishing.com
For customer service and orders:
Toll-Free 1-888-313-2665

Visit us on the Internet at http://www.arcadiapublishing.com

*To Mom and Dad for sharing their affinity for Sanders and keeping me
supplied with jars of milk chocolate hot fudge during my years away*

CONTENTS

ACKNOWLEDGMENTS

Special thanks to Diane Lynch, known as the Sanders Lady at Morley Brands LLC. A former Sanders store manager and director of retail sales, Lynch is now marketing manager for Morley Brands. Sanders chocolate flows in her blood. I also am grateful to John "Jack" Sanders for lending rare photographs and sharing anecdotes about his great-grandfather Fred Sanders and the family business.

INTRODUCTION

No other confectionery in Detroit stirs up as many delectable memories as Sanders. For more than 130 years, Sanders has been a staple on the Motor City's menu, with its incomparable hot fudge cream puff and ice-cream toppings, one-of-a-kind bumpy cake, and fragile honeycomb chips (not to mention a host of other caramel- and cream-filled chocolates). What would Easter in Detroit be without a foiled chocolate purple bunny? Or Christmas without raspberry stufties, those unusual hard candy raspberries stuffed with Sanders's own raspberry puree?

It is difficult to imagine Detroit without Sanders. The company has been around for generations, tracing its beginnings to a young confectioner's dream, a barrel of borrowed sugar, and a leased shop on Woodward Avenue where the J. L. Hudson's block would later rise. From that humble beginning in 1875, the quality of the German-born Fred Sanders's chocolates was never debated, but the struggling businessman—who often worked into the night making chocolates at his home with his wife, Rosa Conrad—strived to prove himself. A year later, he relocated his cream soda and chocolate business closer to Detroit's business district, moving south on Woodward Avenue to the corner of Michigan Avenue. There, his Pavilion of Sweets flourished and Sanders secured his role as Detroit's confectioner.

For a long time, Detroiters took pride in Fred Sanders's invention of the ice-cream soda. Sanders stumbled upon the concoction by accident, serving the mixture to late-night customers he did not want to disappoint at that first shop on Woodward at Gratiot Avenues. Time has since proven that the ice-cream soda was created elsewhere, but Sanders is given credit for introducing the delight to Detroiters and helping the treat gain widespread popularity. Sanders continued to serve ice-cream sodas for decades, but Detroiters fell in love with a long list of other concoctions, especially the hot fudge cream puff. Who created this treat remains unknown, but the "cream puff hot fudge" shows up on some of Sanders earliest menus. Sanders did not enter the baking business until 1913.

While Fred Sanders, or Grandpa Sanders as he was affectionately called, enjoyed his company's success, he could not have imagined the heights his small company—not to mention a bustling Detroit—would reach in the ensuing decades. As the automobile industry stretched Detroit, Sanders expanded, too. By the time of its 50th anniversary, Sanders had seven locations in Detroit and maintained an office, store, and factory at Woodward Avenue and Henry Street, a structure that survived until 2006, when it was razed for Super Bowl XL. In the 1930s and 1940s, Sanders expanded into the suburbs and its growth meant the construction of a modern 400,000-square-foot factory in Highland Park. At the company's peak, in the 1970s, Sanders products were sold at 100 locations in and around Detroit, including J. L. Hudson's, grocery stores, and retail outlets.

Unfortunately, Sanders encountered bumpy roads in the 1980s, filing bankruptcy and changing hands. By the mid-1990s, Sanders stores had disappeared from the Detroit landscape and the future looked bleak. But another Detroit confectioner, Morley Brands LLC, bought the brand in the early 21st century. Responding to Detroiters' cravings—and affection and nostalgia—for Sanders, Morley began remarketing Sanders candy, ice-cream toppings, and baked goods. The company also opened a Sanders Candy and Dessert Shop at Laurel Park Place Mall in Livonia. On the heels of that success, a second Sanders shop was opened in 2005 in Grosse Pointe. At press time, Morley had plans to open yet another store in Birmingham and to renovate the Rochester Morley's retail store as a Sanders store, complete with a contemporary soda fountain.

It is no wonder. The affection and loyalty Detroiters have long felt for Sanders has never waned. Even now, years after all the original Sanders stores have disappeared from the Detroit landscape, generations recall standing two and three deep behind the crowded lunch counter, waiting for a stool and a tuna salad or egg salad sandwich. For many Detroit-area children, stopping by Sanders for an ice-cream sundae, a chocolate milk shake, or a hot fudge cream puff was a treat after shopping with mom or dad, visiting the dentist or doctor, or after school or piano lessons. And everyone, it seems, favors a different Sanders product: caramel tea cake, hot turkey sandwich with mashed potatoes and gravy, almond tea ring, colonial buttercream cake, date nut bars, and the list goes on and on. And then are memories of swivel stools, marble counters, paper cone cups, and delectable chocolates, especially the pecan titans and honeycomb chips.

For Detroit, Sanders was more than just an ice-cream and candy shop. It was a meeting place for generations. The Sanders catalog of products was and remains a part of our everyday life and of our special events.

In the following pages, you will discover a small vestige of Sanders's long and amazing history. Some of you will be disappointed that photographs of your favorite stores in Detroit and the suburbs were not included. Unfortunately, these photographs, if they exist, are in private hands and were not available for use in this book. Thanks to the foresight of Diane Lynch, a former Sanders employee who now markets the brand for Morley's, a wealth of Sanders historic photographs and menus were available for this book.

One

THE SANDERS FAMILY

YOUNG CONFECTIONER. This is an early photograph of Frederick Sanders Schmidt, who would become Detroit's favorite confectioner. Schmidt chose to use his middle name when he went into business because he did not want to appear to compete with his father, Albin Schmidt, a successful baker in downstate Illinois. Sanders studied his craft in Germany, Philadelphia, and Chicago before opening his first store in Detroit in 1875.

GRANDPA SANDERS. Fred Sanders was in his 60s when this photograph was taken sometime after 1910. By then he was a successful Detroit businessman—the owner of the Palace of Sweets on Woodward Avenue. The confectioner was born in Germany, but his family moved to the United States when Sanders was a toddler. The family settled in Peru, Illinois. Sanders returned to Germany to study confectionery and opened his first shop in Frankfurt in 1868. He married a cousin, Rosa Conrad, and returned to America, where he practiced confectionery in Philadelphia and Chicago. He eventually opened his own shop in Chicago, but it was destroyed by the Great Fire of 1871. According to family lore, Sanders ran ahead of the fire to get home to rescue his pregnant wife. They fled their home with Sanders pulling his wife in a carriage.

FIRST STORE. In June 1875, Fred Sanders opened his first confectionery on Woodward Avenue near State Street. An announcement in the Detroit Free Press noted that "He is a practical confectioner, has a handsome place, and will devote his entire attention to customers." Sluggish business prompted the ambitious confectioner to move closer to Detroit's bustling business district the next year. (Courtesy of Jack Sanders.)

EARLY STAFF. A middle-aged Fred Sanders is seated in the center of this portrait with employees of an early store, probably the Pavilion of Sweets. Son Charles is standing on the far right. Son Edwin is seated below his father. The first stores sold only ice cream and candy. On a hot summer day in 1875, Sanders concocted the ice-cream soda. The libation's creation would later be credited to Robert Green, a soda fountain manufacturer from Philadelphia. (Courtesy of Jack Sanders.)

EDWIN SANDERS. Edwin Sanders, the second child of Fred Sanders and Rosa Conrad Sanders, was born in 1874, before the family moved to Detroit. He was the only one of the couple's four children to live well into adulthood. Their first child, Frederick Sanders, was born and died in 1870. Edwin eventually became a partner in the successful and growing family business.

FAMILY PORTRAIT. Fred Sanders and his family pose at their home on Woodward Avenue at Warren Avenue around 1900. The woman seated next to Sanders is Lucy Penning, his daughter-in-law. Her husband, Charles Sanders, is standing behind the sofa. Daughter Ella Sanders is standing next to the sofa. The young boy is grandson Frederick W. Sanders. Rosa Conrad, an invalid later in life, is seated on the far left.

ANOTHER PORTRAIT. The Sanders family moved frequently while living in Detroit. The location of this *c.* 1900 portrait is unknown. Fred and Rosa Conrad Sanders are seated in the far right corner. Son Charles, who possessed a passion for theater and frequented the Detroit Opera House, sits below his father. Edwin is seated at the top of the steps. Grandson Frederick W. Sanders is seated his right. The others are unidentified.

14

COMMUNITY AFFAIR. In this early 1900s photograph, a dapper and elderly Fred Sanders participates in a community fund-raiser. An unidentified woman is pinning something on his lapel. Upon opening his shop in Detroit, Sanders adhered to several principles, including using only the finest ingredients in his confections, closing on Sundays and holidays (he believed those days should be spent with family), and community involvement.

DETROIT PARADE. With his horseless carriage decorated in garland and flowers, Fred Sanders, daughter-in-law Lucy Penning, and grandson Frederick are ready to join a parade celebrating a Detroit event. Sanders was among the first in the city to own a horseless carriage. One day the automobile became stuck in reverse, but Sanders drove it backwards all the way home to Warren Avenue from his Woodward Avenue store.

JOHN MILLER. John Miller, the widower of Sanders's daughter, Ella, who died in 1906, became instrumental in growing the Sanders business. He was known in Detroit as "the great merchandiser." Grandpa Sanders reportedly persuaded his son-in-law to work for him rather than Colonel Goebel, a Detroit beer brewer. Miller was at the helm when Sanders incorporated in 1930.

FREDERICK W. SANDERS. The grandson of founder Frederick Sanders and the son of Charles Sanders and Lucy Penning, Frederick W. Sanders was born in 1895. He became president of the company in 1954, upon the death of John Miller. He remained president until the early 1960s, when he was succeeded by his lifelong friend and business associate Charles H. Welch Jr.

John "Jack" Sanders. The son of Frederick W. Sanders, Jack Sanders began his long career in the family business in the cost accounting department at the Highland Park headquarters, after graduating with a major in math from Amherst College. He became company president in 1963. His daily ritual included walking the plant floor. He became familiar with nearly everyone, and employees often shared photographs of family members, special events, and their summer cottages. He retired as president in 1979.

On a Plant Tour. Jack Sanders serves ice cream to a pair of local Girl Scouts on a tour of the company's Highland Park plant in the mid-1970s. The threesome posed in the plant's ice-cream department. Unlike most large ice-cream producers, Sanders used the batch processing method, with each flavor formulated separately in small batch pasteurizers. Other producers made one flavor—vanilla—and added flavors, nuts, and fruits.

Two

The Pavilion of Sweets

PAVILION OF SWEETS. Taken from across the street from old city hall, this is an early photograph of the Pavilion of Sweets, Sanders's second location on Woodward Avenue. Fred Sanders relocated his confectionery in 1876, hoping his business would improve in the bustling central business district. Note that the canopy advertises ice cream soda water, a concoction the company helped popularize in Detroit.

FUTURE SANDERS CORNER. Taken in the mid-1870s, this photograph of Detroit's bustling core makes it clear why Fred Sanders wanted to relocate his struggling confectionery. The old city hall is on the left, and J. L. Hudson company has opened along Woodward Avenue, a site that would eventually house yet another incarnation of Sanders. The Soldiers and Sailors Monument in the foreground was relocated in the early 21st century to make room for Detroit's new Campus Martius Park.

SANDERS PAVILION. With its striped awnings and Mosque-like roof, the Pavilion of Sweets became the center of Detroit's social and political life. The Pavilion of Sweets was a favorite rendezvous of the after-theater crowd and a regular stopping place for the Detroit Baseball Club. Detroiters also made it a point to bring out-of-town visitors to Sanders for one of the "best ice cream sodas in town."

AUXILIARY FOUNTAIN. This served as the auxiliary fountain in the popular Pavilion of Sweets. Until 1913, Sanders's business included only ice cream and candies. Fred Sanders had concocted his legendary first ice-cream soda a quarter-century earlier when the milk and cream turned sour one busy afternoon. Not wanting to disappoint his customers, Sanders substituted ice cream, and the drink was an immediate success.

WORLD'S FAIR FOUNTAIN. An attraction at the Columbian Exposition in Chicago in 1893, the so-called World's Fair Fountain dominates the back wall. Fred Sanders purchased the fountain for $5,000. The Pavilion of Sweet's first manager, William Deckert Sr., stands near the ornate fountain. The unidentified woman on the right is staffing a floral concession. Sanders rented the concession to a local florist. The archway leads to an addition. Business was so good, Sanders purchased the neighboring Fisher Block for an expansion.

SANDERS EMPLOYEES. Sanders family members and store employees pose for a photograph on the Woodward Avenue side of the Pavilion of Sweets. Grandpa Sanders is standing at the right side of the door. Son Charles is standing next to him. Edwin Sanders is second from the left,

standing next to store manager William Deckert Sr. The familiar striped awnings have been drawn for the photograph.

SYRUP TANKS. In the basement of the Pavilion of Sweets, Edwin Sanders stands next to the syrup tanks. The other two men and the boy in the photograph are unidentified. A flat table, for candy making, can be seen in the foreground.

GRAND ARMY ENCAMPMENT. In 1891, the Grand Army of the Republic met in Detroit. During their encampment and parade along Woodward Avenue, the Civil War veterans were regular customers at the Pavilion of Sweets. With its striped awnings, the Pavilion of Sweets is visible on the left. During the week of the encampment, the Pavilion of Sweets served thousands of ice-cream sodas, according to company lore.

ELECTRIC MOTOR. Sanders was one the first companies in Detroit to use electric motors. This motor has been hooked up to an ice crusher, used in the ice-cream-making process. Unfortunately, the electric motor had a tendency to break down. Frustrated by the inconvenience, Grandpa Sanders was about to get rid of the motor until the Edison Illuminating Company sent over a young mechanic to fix it. The mechanic was Henry Ford. The motor worked well after his tinkering.

CANDY PRODUCTION. Sanders employees made chocolates and other confections on the second floor of the Fisher Block addition. Continued growth would eventually prompt Sanders to build a factory next to one of its future stores, on Woodward Avenue at Henry Street.

SODA FOUNTAIN. This impressive soda fountain was located in the Fisher Block addition. Through the archway on the left, the World's Fair Fountain, as the fountain became known, can be seen. Although Detroiters enjoyed their first ice-cream soda in the summer of 1875, the concoction remained a novelty to much of the country in 1893, the time of the Chicago fair. The World's Fair Fountain eventually became dilapidated and was discarded.

ADDITION INTERIOR. The fluted columns, wall murals, and decorative ceiling matched the elegance of the main Pavilion of Sweets space. In the archway (in the fair right corner), the end of the soda fountain is visible.

Three

ALONG WOODWARD
AVENUE

PALACE OF SWEETS. After spending a short time at 180 Woodward Avenue during the construction of Detroit's first skyscraper, the Majestic Building, Fred Sanders returned to the block that made him a success. Occupying the former J. L. Hudson's building, he opened the Palace of Sweets. This photograph was taken shortly after Sanders occupied the building in 1896.

SANDERS ANNEX. Returning to the old block proved to be another good move for Sanders. This complex would undergo several renovations over the years to make room for candy production, a cafeteria, and a bakery as the company continued to grow. The location would become known as the Downtown Store, and Sanders would occupy the site until the 1980s, when the store closed. A fire in 1956 destroyed the top three floors, but Sanders renovated the gutted building and added a more contemporary facade. Probably built sometime after the Civil War, the structure was shaky. The crooked floors came in handy at tax assessment time. After seeing an orange roll across the slanting floor, the assessor lowered the building's tax value, according to company lore.

THE THRONE ROOM. There was no doubt the Palace of Sweets was opulent. Besides being the home to the famous World's Fair Fountain, Fred Sanders's newest shop replicated the throne room of Ludwig II, the Mad King of Bavaria. No one knows why Sanders chose that décor. Perhaps Sanders intended to pay homage to the country of his birth and the site of his formal training in confectionery. (Courtesy of Jack Sanders.)

BULK CANDY COUNTERS. In this photograph from the 1930s or 1940s, a variety of chocolates, caramels, taffy, and other candies are displayed at the Palace of Sweets. A soda fountain sits in the rear of the store. Sanders's stores were constructed using the finest building materials. Note the marble foundation of the candy counters and marble floors. A portrait of Fred Sanders, who died in 1913, hangs on the rear wall.

SODA FOUNTAIN. The stairs in the foreground lead to a basement cafeteria—sandwiches were eaten downstairs. By the 1930s and 1940s, the Palace of Sweets had been remodeled. A sign on a stairway display case urges customers to visit the bakery department. Grandpa Sanders, whose father was a commercial baker and who studied baking in Germany, decided to return to that love in 1912. Unfortunately, he died before baking became standard in Sanders shops.

LOOKING TOWARD WOODWARD AVENUE. By the time of this photograph in the 1930s or 1940s, the Sanders downtown store had electricity. While not quite as ornate as the original Palace of Sweets, the store retained a sense of elegance and was long a favorite of Detroit's downtown workers and Woodward Avenue shoppers. Note the decorative ceiling, elaborate lights, and marble counter tops.

A SECOND WOODWARD STORE. Outgrowing the manufacturing facilities at the Palace of Sweets, the company built a new three-story building at 2465 Woodward Avenue at Henry Street for both the factory and the store. At the time, the 24,000 square feet of manufacturing was deemed to be adequate for years to come. However, the company quickly outgrew the space and added three more floors to the structure in 1919.

CANDY PRODUCTION. The company's first real factory was built adjacent to the Woodward Avenue store at Henry Street. Here employees are preparing creams for dipping. Workers dipped the bottoms of the creams in chocolate and then placed them on the conveyor belt. The creams were coated with chocolate as they moved through the dipping machine. Notice the chocolate on the woman's hands at the left of the photograph.

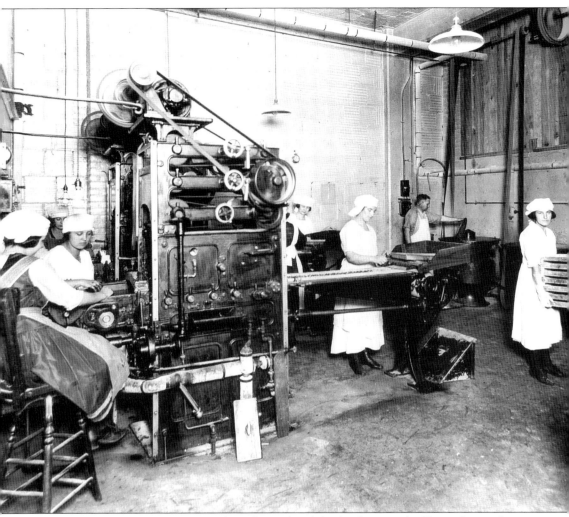

DIPPING CHOCOLATE. White-capped employees hand dip bonbons at the Henry Street plant. This production was a far cry from Sanders candy making in 1875, Fred Sanders worked all day and then trudged to his home on Napoleon Street, where he and his wife, Rosa Conrad Sanders, made candy well into the night for the next day.

DELIVERY TRUCK. An early Sanders delivery truck used to deliver candy and baked goods to Sanders's nearly dozen stores by the late 1920s. This photograph was taken near Cass Park. By this time, the company had three or four delivery trucks. Never mind the No. 17 on the door panel; the company's Henry Street site could only accommodate a of couple trucks. (Courtesy of Jack Sanders.)

WOODWARD AND HENRY STREET STORE, AROUND 1915. With a keen eye for real estate, John Miller purchased the whole block, and a factory was built adjacent to the store, providing the company with 127,000 square feet of space. By this time, Sanders had nine retail stores, either owned or leased in various parts of the city. This structure survived until its razing for Super Bowl XL in 2006.

WOODWARD AND THE BOULEVARD. In 1919, Sanders decided to expand into the northern section of the city and opened this store at Grand Boulevard and Woodward Avenue in the Henry Building. It was Sanders's first venture away from the downtown area. Business at the store was so brisk that the company opened yet another store in 1920 in the Dime Bank Building.

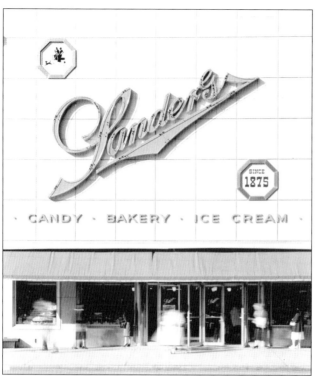

DOWNTOWN STORE. The former Palace of Sweets is a modern three-story building after a fire destroyed the original building in 1956. The new building contained 6,400 square feet of space on two floors and included a cafeteria with table and counter seating for 130 people in the basement. Sanders had occupied the Woodward Avenue site since 1896.

WOODWARD STREETSCAPE. The new Sanders modern exterior motif featured a stainless steel and gray facade. The signature Sanders sign was in tangerine. The store's interior featured shades of black, tangerine, gray, and brown. The store contained self-service for candy, a bakery, and packaged ice cream on the first floor. There also was a stand-up fountain for quick service.

Four

HOLIDAYS AND MILESTONES

THANKSGIVING PARADE. This 1937 photograph shows the Sanders float in the annual J. L. Hudson's Thanksgiving Day Parade. Marking its 62nd year, the Sanders float depicted the original ice-cream soda fountain at its first store. Sanders frequently sponsored floats in the annual holiday parade over the decades.

94110

SWEETEST DAY, 1928. A variety of Sanders candy is featured in this window display advertising Sweetest Day on October 13. Over the years, Sanders has been blamed for creating Sweetest Day to promote candy sales, but the holiday traces its origins to a Cleveland candy maker who gave chocolates and candies to orphans and disadvantaged people.

SWEETEST DAY, 1929. In another Sweetest Day window display, a variety of Sanders boxed chocolates were arrayed to entice customers.

VALENTINE'S DAY. Sanders held contests to see which managers could create the best window displays during holidays and special promotions. This 1929 Valentine's Day display won second prize in the National Window Trimming Contest.

EASTER DISPLAY. While Sanders boxed chocolates and other candies were the focal point of displays, the decorator of this 1930 Easter display incorporated bunny rabbits, flowers, and Easter scenes.

MOTHER'S DAY. This undated photograph shows a Mother's Day window display at an unidentified Sanders store. Note the copy of *Whistler's Mother* in the center of the display.

FOURTH OF JULY. An undated photograph of a Fourth of July display is seen at one of the Sanders stores.

CHRISTMAS DISPLAY, 1928. This elaborate holiday window display promotes a variety of Sanders baked goods amid garland, wreathes, a miniature Santa Claus, a church, and a reindeer-drawn sleigh with Santa at the helm. This photograph also provides a glimpse of the store's interior.

THREE WISE MEN. This elaborate Christmas window display probably adorned the Woodward Avenue at Henry Street store before World War II. The three wise men—John Miller, Frederick W. Sanders, and Edwin Sanders—are depicted as confectioners, each behind a soda fountain and bakery counter. The miniatures were made out of sugar.

SEVENTY YEARS. When Sanders marked its 70th anniversary in 1945, just before the end of World War II, a variety of longtime Detroit businesses celebrated the important event with displays honoring the venerable company and other milestones in the city's history. While congratulating Sanders, this exhibit notes the history of electric service in the city.

4617 - 11

THE SAME YEAR. Michigan Bell Telephone honors Sanders with a display that notes that the same years the confectioner was founded in Detroit, Alexander Graham Bell invented the telephone. Two years later, in 1877, the first telephones were introduced in Michigan.

OLD TIMER. The window of Sanders's Highland Park store notes the company's 70 years of service with portraits of Fred Sanders and photographs of company stores. It is unclear who or what "From One Old Timer To Another" is referring to.

ANOTHER ERA. This Sanders store celebrates the occasion with a display harking back to another era, the decade in which the first Sanders store was founded in 1875. The framed sign in the window is a congratulatory letter from Michigan Consolidated Gas Company.

END OF WAR. Sanders marked the end of World War II with photocopies of *Detroit Free Press* front pages from wars over the centuries, including the Battle of Shiloh during the American Civil War and the Armistice in World War I. The framed note of congratulations at the far right is from the *Detroit Free Press*, of course.

MERRY CHRISTMAS BOOK. When this small booklet was published, Sanders boasted 12 stores in Detroit. The company had yet to reach the suburbs, but its selection of boxed chocolates, custom-filled hampers, hard candy, ribbon candy, fruit cakes, candy canes, and plum pudding could be shipped parcel post all over the country and Canada. For 15¢, a special delivery stamp on a package of up to two pounds ensured more rapid handling.

SAY MERRY CHRISTMAS. By the time this Christmas booklet was published, Sanders had 21 stores and products at the J. L. Hudson Company. Its offices were in Highland Park. The usual Christmas favorites were available with ordering instructions located on the last pages of the 30-page booklet.

BEST CHRISTMAS EVER. Rebounding from the Chapter 11 reorganization, Joe Fontana (right), president of Fontana Brothers, and Joe Miazgowicz, sales manager, celebrate the best Christmas sales ever by cutting a cake at the company's annual holiday party. The Fontana brothers, wholesalers of candy, groceries, and tobacco, were brought in as investors to help the struggling company in the early 1980s.

DUO BIRTHDAYS. A special Sanders cake celebrates the company's 108th anniversary and the 85th anniversary of another local institution, Bob-Lo Island, an amusement park. Generations of Detroiters boarded the Bob-Lo boats for a trip down the Detroit River.

THANKSGIVING FLOAT. Sanders's 1986 Thanksgiving Day parade float featured a giant, orange-feathered bird rowing a dish with a spoon. Inside the bowl is an ice-cream sundae.

Five

MENUS

GOOD THINGS TO EAT. By the time this daily menu was published in 1933, Sanders boasted 13 stores, including one outside the city in Dearborn. Sanders products also were sold at the J. L. Hudson Company, the Village Market, and Richards Market.

SANDERS — GOOD THINGS TO EAT

Today's Specials

Friday, November 17, 1933

25c COMBINATIONS

No. 1
Choice of Soup or Tomato Juice
Choice of any 10c Sandwich
Choice of any 5c Beverage
Choice of 10c Dessert

No. 2
Choice of 20c Salad
Choice of any 5c Beverage
Choice of 10c Dessert

Note: This price applies only to the above combinations. Choice is extended to higher priced items at extra charge. Combination luncheon service for one person only—otherwise a la carte.

SPECIAL DESSERT
Boston Cream Pie
10c

SOUPS
Sanders Navy Bean Soup with Boston Brown Bread . . . 10c
Cream of Asparagus Soup 10c
Chicken Bouillon with Noodles . . . 10c

SANDWICHES
Crab Meat with Celery and Pimiento on Dinner Roll . . . 10c
Chopped Egg with Anchovies on White

SANDWICHES
Ham . . . . 10c (rye or white)
Minced Ham . . . 10c (on bun)
Baked Ham . . . 10c (on new white bread)
Chicken Salad Sandwich . . . 10c (white or whole wheat bread)
Sliced Chicken . . . 15c
Egg Salad . . . 10c (on bun)
American Cheese . . . 10c (white bread)
Swiss Cheese . . . 10c (rye bread)
Cream Cheese . . . 10c (whole wheat bread)
Tuna . . . 10c (white or whole wheat bread)
Salmon . . . 10c (white bread)
Half and Half . . . 15c Choice of White Bread, Rolls Graham Crackers or Zwieback

ROLLS

PIES
Fresh Apple . . . 10c
Lemon Fluff . . . 10c
Custard . . . 10c
Peach . . . 10c
Pumpkin Pie with Whipped Cream . 10c
Hot Mince Meat Pie . 10c With Ice Cream 5c Extra

LAYER CAKES
10c per cut
Chocolate
Cocoanut
Butterscotch
Chocolate Pecan Loaf

Cup Cakes per order . 10c

ICE CREAMS
Vanilla . . . 10c
Chocolate . . . 10c
Strawberry . . . 10c
Mixed Ice Cream . 10c (Portion for Children 5c)

Orange Sherbet . 10c

ICE CREAM SODAS 10c
Chocolate   Vanilla
Lemon   Maple
     Root Beer

SUNDAES
Chocolate . . . 15c
Marshmallow . . 15c
Chocolate Marshmallow . 15c
Butterscotch . . . 15c
Hot Fudge . . . 15c
Hot Bittersweet . 15c
Pecan Nut . . . 20c (with any flavor)
Walnut Sundae . 20c (with any flavor)
Salted Peanut . 20c (with any flavor)
Banana Split . . 20c
Pineapple . . . 15c
Cherry . . . 15c
Black Raspberry . 15c
Strawberry . . . 15c
Parfait . . . 20c

CRUSHED FRUIT SODAS 10c
Pineapple   Cherry
Black Raspberry

BEVERAGES
Coffee 5c
Tea 5c
Milk 5c
Hot Malted Milk . 15c
Hot Chocolate with Cookies . . 10c
Orangeade . . . 10c
Malted Milks . . 10c (with egg 5c extra)
Milk Shakes . . 10c (with egg 5c extra)
Grape Juice . . 15c
Tomato Juice . . 10c
Pineapple Juice . 10c

BREAKFAST
Orange Juice . . 10c
Tomato Juice . . 10c
Prunes . . . 10c
     with Cream . . 15c
Cereals with Cream . 10c
Pep, Corn Flakes, Bran, Shredded Wheat, Grape Nuts, Rice Crispies
Rolls and Butter . . 5c
Cinnamon Rolls and

ANNOUNCING
that
Sanders Downtown Store
1037 Woodward Avenue
Next to Majestic Building
will be
open until
11:00 p.m.
Beginning Monday November 20th

Have your supper at Sanders before the movies. One Hot Supper special served daily

We Suggest
Chicken a la King en Pattie Shell with Roll and Coffee . . . 25c
Creamed Tuna on Chinese Noodles with Roll and Coffee . . . 25c
Veal Pie with Carrots, Roll and Coffee

MENU, 1933. Printed daily menus began appearing in Sanders stores as far back as the 1920s. Besides the standard luncheon counter fare and ice-cream treats, the menu highlighted daily specials. This November 17 menu also announced that Sanders's Downtown Store, at 1037 Woodward Avenue, would be open until 11:00 p.m. beginning the following Monday. The additional store hours were Sanders's way of helping President Roosevelt's Recovery Program by giving work to more people.

SUNDAE CUPS. The Sanders sundae cups displayed on the cover of this 1937 menu were popular with catering events in the 1930s and 1940s. With its vast selection of baked goods and luncheon foods, Sanders catered many functions. The ice cream was packed in Dixie cups, and customers could choose from six flavors: chocolate, strawberry, raspberry, cherry, pineapple, and chocolate marshmallow.

Sanders

GOOD THINGS TO EAT

BREAKFAST MENU

TODAY'S SPECIALS
April 3, 1937
Saturday

Sanders

GOOD THINGS TO EAT

· · DESSERTS · ·

LUNCHEON AND SUPPER SPECIALS 30¢

Chop Suey on Chinese Noodles,
Roll and Coffee

SOUPS

Sanders Chicken Soup with Julienne Vegetables — 10c
Sanders Cream of Spinach Soup — 10c

SALADS

Stuffed Egg Salad with Ham and Rolls — 25c

Fruit Salad and Rolls — 30c
Head Lettuce Salad with Choice of Dressing and Rolls — 30c

SANDWICHES

Chopped Roast Veal with Pickle on White Bread — 35c
Olive, Celery and Nut on Cracked Wheat Bread — 10c
Minced Ham with Mushrooms on White Bread — 40c
Chicken Salad with Peas on French Bread — 35c

DESSERT

Chocolate Salted Peanut Sundae — 15c

ICE CREAMS

Pistachio — 10c Chocolate Marshmallow — 10c
Butter Pecan — 10c Pineapple Sherbet — 10c

All Prices Subject to Michigan Retail Sales Tax

MENU, 1937. This April 3, 1937, menu varies little from the 1933 menu. Many of the items are priced the same. This menu includes the company's famous devil's food buttercream cake, now known as the bumpy cake. The cream puff hot fudge, known to Detroiters as the hot fudge cream puff, was listed under pastries and sold for 15¢.

MENU, 1941. Sanders began by selling just ice-cream sodas and candy, but over the years its menu expanded to include luncheon fare and baked goods. According to this 1941 menu, Sanders served breakfast, lunch, and supper. This menu advertised Sanders Bridge Luncheon, a complete luncheon for one bridge table—chicken salad, rolls, cookies, ice cream, and candy.

BREAKFAST

Fruits — Juices

Tomato Juice	15c and 20c
Orange Juice	20c and 30c
Grapefruit	15c
Fresh Grapefruit (Half)	15c
Pineapple Slice	15c
Prunes . . 15c Apricots	15c
Peaches . 25c Pears	20c

(Cream, Small Pitcher 5c)

Hot or Cold Cereals

With Large Pitcher of Milk	20c
With Large Pitcher of Cream	25c
With Bottle of Milk	25c

Fried Cakes
Sweet Rolls — Toast

Fried Cake	8c
(Plain or Sugared)	
Glazed Doughnut	8c
French Cruller	10c
Danish Butter Twist	15c
Butterscotch Sweet Roll	15c
Cinnamon Roll	10c
(Butter, Pat 2c)	
BUTTERED TOAST	15c
Buttered English Muffin	15c
Crackers (1 pkg.) with Butter	5c
(Extra Butter, Pat 2c)	

Beverages

Coffee or Tea	10c
Instant Sanka	15c
Milk . . 15c Chocolate Milk	15c
Hot Chocolate	15c
with Whipped Cream	20c
Ginger Ale, Coca Cola or Root Beer	10c
Malted Milk (all flavors)	25c
Milk Shake (all flavors)	25c
with Egg, 10c extra	

NO TIPPING, PLEASE

LUNCHEON AND SUPPER
MONDAY, MARCH 28, 1960

SPECIAL PLATES

Baked Macaroni and Cheese in Casserole	40c
Juicy Chopped Barbecued Beef Sandwich	40c
with Crisp Potato Chips	45c
Sanders Old Fashioned Beef Stew on Hot Buttered Noodles	50c

SALADS

TUNA VEGETABLE SALAD	50c
PINEAPPLE AND COTTAGE CHEESE SALAD	30c
Potato Salad . 25c Large Fruit Salad . 55c Fruit Salad .	35c
Head Lettuce Salad . . 20c Cabbage Salad	20c
Sliced Tomato Salad . . 20c Cottage Cheese	15c

ROLLS

Sesame Seed Kaiser Roll 10c   Dinner Roll 10c   Cherry Muffin 10c
Cloverleaf Roll 10c   Raisin Bran Muffin 10c   Flaky Butter Roll 10c
(Extra Butter, Pat 2c)

SOUPS

Lima Bean Soup with Ham	20c and 30c
Cream of Corn Soup (Meatless)	20c and 30c

SANDWICHES

1. Sliced Roast Beef on White Bread	40c
2. Chopped Egg with Olives on Whole Wheat Bread	35c
3. Turkey Liver and Egg on Rye Bread	35c

Sliced Ham	40c	Chopped Roast Beef	40c
(White or Rye Bread)		(White Bread)	
Minced Ham with		Turkey Salad	50c
Celery and Relish	40c	(White or Whole Wheat Bread)	
(on Bun)		Lettuce and Tomato	30c
Egg Salad	35c	(White or Whole Wheat Bread)	
(White Bread)		Tuna with Celery	40c
Sliced American Cheese	30c	(White or Whole Wheat Bread)	
(Rye Bread)		Sliced Swiss Cheese	35c
		(Pumpernickel Bread)	

FEATURED DESSERTS

	2 Scoop Serving	Single Scoop Serving
Hot Caramel Fudge Sundae		30c
Cherry Iced Silver Loaf Cake with Ice Cream		25c
Pineapple Angel Cream Pie	25c	
Blueberry Pie with Ice Cream		30c
Today's Feature	25c	20c
Almond Toffee Ice Cream	25c	20c
Cocoanut Milk Chocolate Ice Cream	25c	20c
Additional Scoop 10c		

DESSERTS

Sundaes

2 Scoops 30c; Single 25c

Chocolate	Cherry	Pineapple
Strawberry	Maple	Butterscotch
Red Raspberry		Marshmallow
	Chocolate Marshmallow	

2 Scoops 35c; Single 30c

Hot Fudge	Hot Bittersweet
Nut Sundaes 10c extra	
Banana Split	55c
Cream Puff Hot Fudge	35c

Additional Scoop or Topping 10c extra;
Whipped Cream 10c extra

Ice Cream Sodas

2 Scoops 30c; Single 25c

Vanilla	Cherry Maple
Pineapple	Lemon Root Beer
Chocolate	Strawberry
Red Raspberry	Ginger Ale Float

Ice Creams

2 Scoops 25c; Single 20c

Vanilla, Chocolate or
Banana Nut

Pies 20c

Apple	Custard	Lemon Meringue
Blueberry		Cherry
	Pineapple Angel Cream 25c	

Layer Cakes 20c

Caramel	New England Cocoanut
Double Chocolate	Fudge Iced
Colonial Buttercream 25c	
Devilsfood Buttercream 25c	

PASTRIES 20c

CUP CAKES 15c

DAILY MENU COVERS. These daily menu covers from the 1950s and 1960s promote Sanders baked goods—an assortment of cookies and meringue ice-cream cake—and remind customers of upcoming holidays, Easter and Christmas. Even by March 1960, little had changed on the Sanders daily menu except for prices. Ice-cream sodas cost 25¢ for one scoop and 30¢ for two scoops. Pies and layer cakes were just 20¢. The famous cream puff hot fudge, as it was called on the menu, cost 35¢. Sanders stopped printing daily menus in the 1940s.

BREAKFAST

Fruits — Juices

Tomato Juice	. . . .	15c and 20c
Orange Juice	. . . .	20c and 30c
Grapefruit	. . . . . .	15c
Pineapple Slice	. . . .	15c
Prunes . . 15c	Apricots . .	15c
Peaches . 25c	Pears . . .	20c

(Cream. Small Pitcher 5c)

Hot or Cold Cereals

With Large Pitcher of Milk . . .	20c
With Large Pitcher of Cream . .	25c
With Bottle of Milk	25c

Fried Cakes
Sweet Rolls — Toast

Fried Cake	8c
(Plain or Sugared)	
Glazed Doughnut	8c
French Cruller	10c
Danish Butter Twist	15c
Cinnamon Circle Sweet Roll . .	10c
Cinnamon Roll	10c
(Butter. Pat 2c)	
BUTTERED TOAST	15c
Buttered English Muffin . . .	15c
Crackers (1 pkg.) with Butter . .	5c
(Extra Butter, Pat 2c)	

Beverages

Coffee or Tea	10c
Instant Sanka	15c
Milk . . 15c Chocolate Milk .	15c
Milk made with Sanders	
Chocolate Syrup	25c
Hot Chocolate	15c
with Whipped Cream . . .	20c
Ginger Ale, Coca Cola or	
Root Beer	10c
Malted Milk (all flavors) . . .	25c
Milk Shake (all flavors) . . .	25c
with Egg, 10c extra	

NO TIPPING, PLEASE

LUNCHEON AND SUPPER

TUESDAY, JANUARY 3, 1961

SPECIAL PLATES

Louisiana Macaroni Casserole	50c
Beef Pattie with Fluffy Mashed Potatoes and Brown Gravy . .	50c
Juicy Chopped Barbecued Beef Sandwich	40c
with Crisp Potato Chips	45c
Fluffy Mashed Potatoes with Brown Gravy	15c

SALADS

TUNA, EGG AND MACARONI SALAD . . .	45c
PEACH AND COTTAGE CHEESE SALAD . . .	30c
Potato Salad . 25c Large Fruit Salad . 55c Fruit Salad .	35c
Head Lettuce Salad . . 20c Cabbage Salad . . .	20c
Sliced Tomato Salad . . 20c Cottage Cheese . . .	15c

ROLLS

Sesame Seed Soft Roll 10c	Dinner Roll 10c
Cherry Muffin 10c Raisin Bran Muffin 10c	Flaky Butter Roll 10c

(Extra Butter, Pat 2c)

SOUPS

Cream of Tomato Soup	20c and 30c
Yellow Split Pea Soup with Bacon . .	20c and 30c

SANDWICHES

1. Sliced Corned Beef on White Bread	40c
2. American Cheese with Dill Pickle and Nuts	
on Pumpernickel Bread	40c
3. Sliced French Meat Loaf on Rye Bread	40c
4. Beef Pattie on Bun	40c

Sliced Ham . . . 40c	Chopped Roast Beef .	40c
(White or Rye Bread)	(White Bread)	
Minced Ham with	Turkey Salad	50c
Celery and Relish . . 40c	(White or Whole Wheat Bread)	
(on Bun)	Lettuce and Tomato . .	30c
	(White or Whole Wheat Bread)	
Egg Salad . . . 35c	Tuna with Celery . . .	40c
(White Bread)	(White or Whole Wheat Bread)	
Sliced American Cheese . 30c	Sliced Swiss Cheese . .	35c
(Rye Bread)	(Pumpernickel Bread)	

	2 Scoop Serving	Single Scoop Serving
FEATURED DESSERTS		
Strawberry Pineapple Crush Sundae	30c	
Fudge Iced Gold Loaf Cake with Ice Cream . . .		25c
Red Raspberry Pie with Ice Cream		30c
Coconut Angel Cream Pie with Ice Cream . . .		35c
Butter Pecan Ice Cream	25c	20c
	Additional Scoop 10c	

DESSERTS

Sundaes

2 Scoops 30c; Single 25c

Chocolate	Cherry	Pineapple
Strawberry	Maple	Butterscotch
Red Raspberry		Marshmallow
	Chocolate Marshmallow	

2 Scoops 35c; Single 30c

Hot Fudge	Hot Bittersweet

Nut Sundaes 10c extra

Banana Split	55c
Cream Puff Hot Fudge	35c

*Additional Scoop or Topping 10c extra;
Whipped Cream 10c extra*

Ice Cream Sodas

2 Scoops 30c; Single 25c

Vanilla	Cherry Maple
Pineapple	Lemon Root Beer
Chocolate	Strawberry
Red Raspberry	Ginger Ale Float

Ice Creams

2 Scoops 25c; Single 20c

Vanilla, Chocolate or
Pecan Milk Chocolate

Pies 20c

Pumpkin	Red Raspberry
Apple Custard	Lemon Meringue
Coconut Angel Cream 25c	

Layer Cakes 20c

Caramel	New England Coconut
	Double Chocolate
Colonial Buttercream	25c
Devilsfood Buttercream Layer .	25c

PASTRIES 20c

CUP CAKES 15c

BREAKFAST

Fruits—Juices

Tomato Juice	15c and 20c
Orange Juice	20c and 30c
Grapefruit	15c
Fresh Grapefruit (Half)	15c
Pineapple Slice	15c
Prunes . . 15c Apricots	15c
Peaches . 25c Pears	20c

(Cream, Small Pitcher 3c)

Hot or Cold Cereals

With Large Pitcher of Milk	20c
With Large Pitcher of Cream	25c

Fried Cakes
Sweet Rolls—Toast

Fried Cake	8c
(Plain or Sugared)	
Glazed Doughnut	8c
Danish Butter Twist	15c
Butterscotch Sweet Roll	15c
Cinnamon Roll	10c
French Cruller	10c
(Butter, Pat 2c)	
BUTTERED TOAST	15c
Buttered English Muffin	15c
Crackers (1 pkg.) with Butter	5c
(Extra Butter, Pat 2c)	

Beverages

Coffee, Tea or Postum	10c
Milk . 15c Chocolate Milk	15c
Hot Chocolate	15c
with Whipped Cream	20c
Ginger Ale, Coca Cola or Root Beer	10c
Malted Milk (all flavors)	25c
Milk Shake (all flavors)	25c
with Egg, 10c extra	

NO TIPPING, PLEASE

LUNCHEON AND SUPPER
TUESDAY, FEBRUARY 17, 1959

SPECIAL PLATES

Corned Beef Hash in Casserole	55c
Hot Meat Loaf Sandwich with Brown Gravy	40c
with Fluffy Mashed Potatoes	50c
Italian Spaghetti with Mushroom Sauce	45c
Fluffy Mashed Potatoes with Brown Gravy	15c

SALADS

TUNA, EGG AND MACARONI SALAD	45c
PINEAPPLE AND COTTAGE CHEESE SALAD	30c
Potato Salad . 25c Large Fruit Salad . 55c Fruit Salad	35c
Head Lettuce Salad . . 20c Cabbage Salad	20c
Sliced Tomato Salad . 20c Cottage Cheese	15c

ROLLS

Dinner Roll . 10c Kaiser Roll . . 10c Raisin Bran Muffin	10c
Luncheon Roll 10c Cherry Muffin . 10c Flaky Butter Roll .	10c

(Extra Butter, Pat 2c)

SOUPS

Cream of Tomato Soup (Meatless)	20c and 30c
Lentil Soup	20c and 30c

SANDWICHES

1. Sliced Corned Beef on White Bread	35c
2. Chopped Ham with Mustard Pickle on Rye Bread	40c
3. Sliced Pinconning Cheese on Pumpernickel Bread	35c

Sliced Ham	40c	Chopped Roast Beef .	40c
(White or Rye Bread)		(White Bread)	
Minced Ham with		Turkey Salad	50c
Celery and Relish . .	40c	(White or Whole Wheat Bread)	
(on Bun)		Lettuce and Tomato . .	30c
Egg Salad	35c	(White or Whole Wheat Bread)	
(White Bread)		Tuna with Celery . . .	40c
Sliced American Cheese .	30c	(White or Whole Wheat Bread)	
(Rye Bread)		Sliced Swiss Cheese . .	35c
		(Pumpernickel Bread)	

FEATURED DESSERTS

	2 Scoop Serving	Single Scoop Serving
Cream Puff Hot Fudge		35c
Devilsfood Buttercream Pastry with Ice Cream		30c
Cherry Pie with Ice Cream		30c
Butter Pecan Ice Cream	25c	20c
Almond Milk Chocolate Ice Cream	25c	20c
Chocolate Chip Ice Cream	25c	20c

Additional Scoop 10c

DESSERTS

Sundaes

2 Scoops 30c; Single 25c

Chocolate	Cherry	Pineapple
Strawberry	Maple	Butterscotch
Red Raspberry		Marshmallow
Chocolate Marshmallow		

2 Scoops 35c; Single 30c

Hot Fudge	Hot Bittersweet
Nut Sundaes 10c extra	
Banana Split	55c
Cream Puff Hot Fudge	55c

Additional Scoop or Topping 10c extra;
Whipped Cream 10c extra

Ice Cream Sodas

2 Scoops 30c; Single 25c

Vanilla	Cherry	Maple
Pineapple	Lemon	Root Beer
Chocolate		Strawberry
Red Raspberry		Ginger Ale Float

Ice Creams

2 Scoops 25c; Single 20c

Vanilla, Chocolate or
Cherry Vanilla

Pies 20c

Apple	Custard	Lemon Meringue
	Cherry	
Chocolate Meringue Cream		

Layer Cakes 20c

Caramel	New England Cocoanut
Double Chocolate	Fudge Iced
Maple Pecan	
Colonial or Devilsfood Buttercream 25c	

PASTRIES 20c

CUP CAKES 15c

LUNCHEON AND SUPPER. Printing daily luncheon and dinner menus was a huge undertaking. Eventually Sanders combined the menus, offering the same fare at lunch and dinner. In the late 1960s, Sanders hired a professional menu design company to create a new permanent menu for its stores. The menus included a daily insert for special soups, sandwiches, entrees, and desserts. Among the new items to be featured were three overstuffed sandwiches—roast beef, corned beef, and ham.

Sundaes

2 Scoops 25c; Single 19c

Additional Scoop 9c

Chocolate	Marshmallow
Chocolate Marshmallow	
Cherry	Red Raspberry
Pineapple	Maple
Strawberry	Butterscotch
Hot Fudge or Hot Bittersweet	

Nut Sundaes (Peanuts, 7c extra;
All Other Nuts, 10c extra)

(With Whipped Cream, 7c extra)

Ice Cream

	2 Scoop Serving	Single Scoop Serving
Vanilla, Chocolate or Cherry Festival	18c	12c
	Additional Scoop 9c	
Cream Puff Hot Fudge 25c	Banana Split	40c

Cakes

Whipped Cream Cake	15c
Devilsfood Buttercream	20c
Double Chocolate	15c
Chocolate	15c
Caramel	15c
New England Cocoanut	15c
Cup Cake	10c

(With Ice Cream, 7c extra)
(With Whipped Cream, 7c extra)

Beverages

Chocolate Milk	15c
Ginger Ale	5c and 10c
Coca Cola	5c and 10c
Root Beer	5c and 10c
Milk Shake (all flavors)	25c
Malted Milks (all flavors)	25c
(with Egg, 5c extra)	
Triple Dip Malted Milk, All Flavors	35c

Ice Cream Sodas

19c

Chocolate	Vanilla
Lemon	Maple
Root Beer	Pineapple
Cherry	Red Raspberry
Strawberry	
Ginger Ale Float	

Pies

Mince	20c
Pumpkin	20c
Lemon Meringue	20c
Custard	20c
Apple	20c
Cherry	20c
Red Raspberry	20c

(With Ice Cream, 7c extra)
(With Whipped Cream, 7c extra)

Pastries

Devilsfood Buttercream	15c
Cherry or Lemon Tart	15c
Blueberry Tart	15c
Strawberry Tart	15c
Southern Pecan Tart	15c
Napoleon Slice	15c
Apple Turnover	15c
Chocolate Custard Puff	15c
Caramel Custard Puff	15c
Whipped Cream Puff	15c

(With Ice Cream, 7c extra)
(With Whipped Cream, 7c extra)

**SPECIAL
2 FRIED CAKES**
choice of
Coffee, Tea
or Milk
18c

**SPECIAL
RED RASPBERRY
PIE a la Mode
25c**

LUNCHEON AND SUPPER

MONDAY, NOVEMBER 30, 1953

SPECIAL PLATES

Ham, Macaroni and Cheese Casserole	55c
Chopped Barbecued Veal Sandwich, Potato Chips	35c
Beef Stew on Buttered Noodles	45c

SOUPS

Potato Bacon Soup	15c
Turkey Mulligatawny Soup	15c

SANDWICHES

1. Sliced Roast Beef on White Bread	40c
2. Chopped Ham and Cheese on Rye Bread	35c
3. Variety: ½ Salmon Salad on White Bread, ½ Egg Salad on Wheat Bread	35c

Sliced Ham	35c	Chopped Roast Beef	35c
(White or Rye Bread)		(White Bread)	
Minced Ham with		Turkey Salad	40c
Celery and Relish	35c	(White or Whole Wheat Bread)	
(On Bun)			
Egg Salad	30c	Lettuce and Tomato	25c
(White Bread)		(White or Whole Wheat Bread)	
Sliced American Cheese	25c	Tuna with Celery	30c
(Rye Bread)		(White or Whole Wheat Bread)	

SALADS

Fruit Salad	50c	Cabbage Salad	15c
Potato Salad	20c	Sliced Tomato Salad	20c
Lettuce and Tomato Salad	35c	Head Lettuce Salad	15c
SALMON AND MACARONI SALAD			50c
Cottage Cheese		15c	

SPECIAL DESSERTS

		2 Scoop Serving	Single Scoop Serving
Hot Cocoanut Fudge Sundae		22c	
Whipped Cream Horn			20c
French Vanilla Ice Cream		18c	12c
Chocolate Chip Ice Cream		18c	12c
		Additional Scoop 9c	

SANDERS EMPLOYEES DO NOT ACCEPT TIPS

CARRY-OUT. In the Sanders stores with fountain service, carry-out service was a big part of lunch. Soups, salads, hot foods, baked goods, desserts, and beverages were available for carry-out. Special-order departments handled orders for wedding, birthday, and special occasion cakes; salads; sandwiches; fruit punch; ice-cream molds and cakes; and party candies.

TODAY'S SUGGESTIONS

REFRESHING SALADS

DELIGHTFUL TUNA SALAD PLATE
Fresh tuna salad on a bed of lettuce
with sliced tomato, hard cooked eggs
and fresh Muffins   .89

Tomato, Egg and Cottage Cheese Salad
Very Refreshing   .59

Cottage Cheese Salad   .25
Zesty Potato Salad   .30
Creamy Cole Slaw Salad   .30
Our Own Bean Salad   .30
Sliced Tomato Salad   .30
Head Lettuce Salad   .30

B

lettuce, me
dressing an
toasted ses
(With frenc

LI'L SANDY
Juicy, Choic
dill pickle o
(With frenc

LI'L SANDY
Juicy, Choic
lettuce, dill
(With frenc

French Frie

OVER S

Thin Sliced

Wafer Thin

HOT SA

HOT FRENCH
best - au jus

FISH-WICH

COLD S

TURKEY SAL
TEEN TWIST
and Lettuce
on a French
MINCED HA

MENU, 1950s. Sanders simplified its menus in the 1950s and used this theme into the early 1960s. With pink, brown, and white tones, this laminated three-page menu was a far cry from the confectioner's menus in the 1930s and 1940s. The menu had been whittled to a few burgers

RS
H

.) Juicy, Choice,
und beef; crisp
Sanders special
slice on
5
reamy cole slaw) .99

ound beef, lettuce,
roll .50
reamy cole slaw) .75
RGER
ound beef, melted cheese,
ndwich roll .60
reamy cole slaw) .85
.30

ED
ICHES

n Style
Beef -
icy .85

Delicious .85

m .79

ICHES

Best Ball Park .35
D BEEF
Chips .65
Roast Beef at its
roll .89
with Potato Chips .55

ICHES

SALAD -
Favorite .55
D - Zesty .50
CHEESE .40
al Recipe .60
eese, Tomato
al Sauce

.60

FOUNTAIN FAVORITES

All of our Fountain
Specialties are made with
Sanders delicious, wonderfully
rich ice cream -
a Tradition of Excellence.

CREAM PUFF HOT FUDGE .55
A superb taste treat - Puff shell filled with
delicious ice cream and smothered with
rich Hot Fudge.

HOT FUDGE SUNDAE .55
Milk Chocolate or Bittersweet
2 Big scoops of Ice Cream - generously covered
with Sanders Hot Fudge or Hot Bittersweet.

SUNDAE .50
Rich Sanders Ice Cream with your choice of
tempting toppings.

Chocolate	**Pineapple**	**Raspberry**
Cherry	**Marshmallow**	**Strawberry**

BANANA SUPREME .65
A delectable combination of ice cream, sliced
bananas, hot fudge, whipped cream and nuts.

ICE CREAM MONDAES .50
A taste tempting new fountain delight -
an ice cream soda topped with Sundae Sauce
and whipped cream. **You must try it.**

THE ORIGINAL ICE CREAM SODA .40
for over 90 years - the pride of Detroit.
Your choice of the following flavors:

Pineapple	**Chocolate**	**Vanilla**
Lemon	**Cherry**	**Red Raspberry**

ICE CREAMS - A large dish of Your Favorite .35

FROM OUR BAKERY

English Muffin .25
Old Fashion Coffee Cake -
Toasted .25
Buttered Old Fashion Toast .25
Our Special Pies .25
Famous Sanders Cake .30
Cake or Pie a la Mode 15c extra

BEVERAGES

Vernors Float .40
Sanders Jubilee Freeze .39
Coffee .15   Milk .15
Hot Chocolate with Whipped Cream .20
Malted Milk .39   Milk Shake .39
Fruit Jubilee .20
Tea — Hot or Iced .15
Coca-Cola .20   Vernors .20

---

and sandwiches—tuna and egg salad were still there. Ice-cream sodas and cream puff hot fudge
remained popular favorites.

61

APPETEASERS

Chilled Tomato Juice	.15
Chilled Orange Juice	.25
Florida Fruit Cup	.30
Choice of Two Soups of the Day (Sanders Homemade)	Bowl .40 Cup. 25

BURGERS AND SUCH

Big Sandy—thick (¼ lb.), juicy, choice, freshly ground beef; crisp lettuce; melted cheese; dill pickle slice on sesame seed roll		.70
		(With french fries and creamy cole slaw)
		.95
Hamburger Diablo—stuffed with relish, pimento, onions and savory sauce	.65	.90
Fry Snack—a delicious filled sandwich (tuna or ham salad) dipped in egg batter and deep-fried to a golden brown	.50	.75
Li'l Sandy—juicy, choice, freshly ground beef; lettuce; dill pickle on sandwich roll	.45	.70
Grilled Frankfurter in hot roll	.35	.60

French Fried Potatoes .30   French Fried Onion Rings .35

BEVERAGES

The Big "O" (our special whipped orange drink made with fresh-frozen orange juice)	.25		
Milk Shakes (Vanilla, Chocolate, Strawberry)	.40	Hot Chocolate with whipped cream	.20
		Coca Cola	.15
Tea—Hot or Iced	.15	Fresca Diet Drink	.15
Coffee .15 Sanka .20		Vernors Ginger Ale	.15
Milk—Chocolate Milk	.15		

SANDWICHES Served with garnish

FOUNTAIN FAVORITES

All of our fountain specialties are made with Sanders' delicious, wonderfully rich ice cream—a tradition of excellence among generations of Detroiters.

Cream Puff Hot Fudge—a superb taste treat—a crisp puff shell filled with ice cream, covered with luscious hot fudge and topped with whipped cream and nuts	.55
Hot Fudge Sundae—two big scoops of ice cream, generously covered with Sanders' scrumptious hot fudge—and topped with whipped cream and nuts	.55
Sundaes—rich Sanders Ice Cream topped with your choice of the following flavors, plus whipped cream and nuts	.55

Hot Bittersweet	Cherry	Raspberry
Strawberry	Pineapple	Chocolate
	Marshmallow	

Banana Supreme—a delectable combination of ice cream, sliced bananas, hot fudge, whipped cream and nuts	.65
Ice Cream Mondaes—a taste-tempting new fountain delight —an ice cream soda topped with sundae sauce and whipped cream. YOU MUST TRY IT	.45
Ice Cream Dish—choice of flavors	.35

COFFEE SHOP MENU. In the 1960s, Sanders used photographs of its salad, sandwich, and dessert offerings to entice customers. Tuna and egg salad sandwiches were still on the menu. Customers were welcomed to their sparkling new Sanders Coffee Shop with this reminder: "You are not expected to tip at Sanders!"

MENU, 1990s. In its last decade, as Sanders Detroiters had loved for more than a century, the menu had been pared considerably. The burgers of earlier decades were largely gone except for a few locations that maintained grills and fryers. Also gone were popular favorites of decades past, the tuna and egg salad sandwiches. Traditional sundaes and the cream puff hot fudge remained. Featured was Bumpity Bliss, devil's food buttercream cake with one scoop of Sanders ice cream and milk chocolate fudge topping. By 1991, the company's heyday had passed, but 16 Sanders stores and restaurants remained in metropolitan Detroit. Its boxed candies, ice cream, and ice-cream toppings were still sold in local grocery stores and other retail stores in southeastern Michigan and neighboring states.

Six

CONFECTIONS

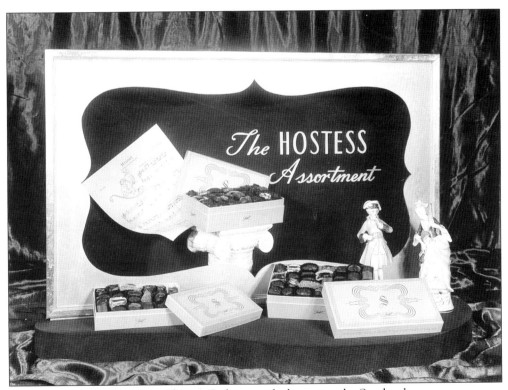

THE HOSTESS ASSORTMENT. This 1947 photograph showcases the Sanders hostess assortment. This collection of boxed chocolates included chocolate-coated fruits, nuts, and creams, plus Figaro cups, sugared almonds, butter almond toffee, and pecan acorns. Milk or dark chocolate coatings were available.

JINGLE. The forerunners of Sanders pecan titans were originally boxed as Jingles. They include chocolate cups containing nuts of some sort. No one recalls how the company came up with the name Jingles for this boxed assortment.

MEADOW MILK CHOCOLATES. Long a staple of the Sanders boxed chocolates collection, this assortment features lighter milk chocolate coatings. The centers include maple pecan, glace pineapple, date, vanilla cream, lemon, pecan cream, tinglings, pecan caramels, almond coconut chips, brazils, walnuts, and others. A variation of the Meadow Milk collection remains available today.

HONEYCOMB CHIPS. A perennial Sanders favorite, the honeycomb chips are shown here in 1950s- and 1960s-era boxes. The honeycomb chip is hardened taffy that has been pulled, shaped, and cut in thin chips. Its name derives from the honeycomb look of over 100 tiny cells in this delicate taffy. The honeycomb chips are still sold under the Sanders brand today.

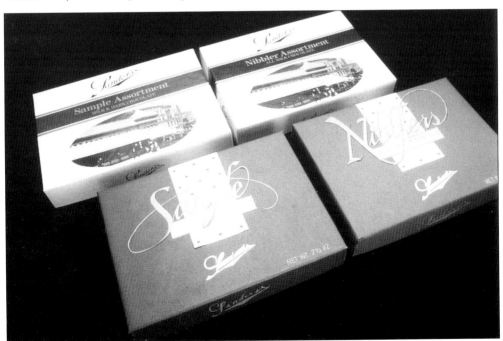

CONCEPT BOXES. Over the years, the covers of the boxed chocolates were updated to reflect changing times. The boxes here were concepts introduced by the marketing staff. They were never used.

BUNNY DISPLAY. No holiday passed without Sanders creating chocolates and candies to mark the occasion. These foiled chocolate bunnies have all been named by a creative Sanders employee. The company's purple-foiled chocolate Easter bunnies have been a Detroit favorite for years.

COLONIAL BUTTERCREAM CAKE. The earliest Sanders stores did not feature baked goods, only sodas and candy. Founder Fred Sanders laid plans to return to his love—baking—in 1912. The company did so after his death in 1913. This early 1900s buttercream recipe was used for Sanders wedding cakes and decorated birthday cakes for generations.

DEVIL'S FOOD BUTTERCREAM CAKE. The company's beloved cake was being baked and served by Sanders as far back as the 1920s. There is no record of how the cake originated, but the combination of confectioner and baker probably created this cake, beloved for its fudge topping. Customers have long called it the bumpy cake.

CARAMEL CAKE. Sanders's old-fashioned caramel cake is another customer favorite. Bakers used sweet cream, pure cane sugar, and real creamery butter, slowed cooked the old-fashioned way, to create this delectable cake. The caramel cake has reappeared in grocery stores and retail shops thanks to the efforts of Morley Candy Makers.

WEDDING CAKES. Sanders's elaborate wedding cakes became a staple after the opening of the Highland Park plant in the 1940s. Cakes could be ordered through any suburban or city retail store and delivered to the hall for the wedding reception. The colonial buttercream wedding cake was a favorite, along with its cherry nut filling. Today Sanders offers an eight-inch colonial buttercream layer cake.

SPECIALTY CAKES. This 1950s-era specialty cake with a Davy Crockett motif (remember the show was popular then) was typical of the efforts Sanders bakers went to please customers. First birthday cakes were a popular specialty cake. Cake decorators would use a photograph of the baby to decorate the cake, using pink or blue to accent the cake, depending on the baby's gender. Seasonal cakes also were popular for parties.

WALNUT RING. Like the Sanders almond ring, the walnut ring was a popular pastry for afternoon tea or breakfast.

SANDERS BREAD. Sanders began baking in 1913, installing one oven and employing two bakers at the Palace of Sweets. From this humble beginning, the Sanders Baking Department prospered, at one time accounting for 35 percent of the company's business.

CREAM CAKES. These cakes were baked in the Highland Park plant and then decorated by workers at Sanders's various stores. Despite their simplicity, the cakes were popular sellers.

BOXED CAKES. With the opening of its Highland Park facility, Sanders had the means to begin mass-producing and packaging its beloved products, including cakes. In 1951, the company began opening candy, bakery, and ice-cream departments in a few C. F. Smith stores. Some featured food service counters like Sanders retail stores, but they were phased out after a few years.

DONUTS. Sanders donuts and cinnamon raisin rolls were walk-in favorites at many stores. At its peak, the company baked 28 varieties of donuts, including plain or sugared fried cakes, twisted fried cakes, and jelly donuts.

COOKIES. Cookies were another walk-in favorite. Popular sellers included the hermit, chocolate chip, peanut butter, and oatmeal-raisin.

CAKES. A variety of cakes are available in this typical Sanders store counter. On display are double chocolate, caramel, and the famous bumpy cake, the devil's food buttercream cake.

BAKERY COUNTER. Women shop for donuts at a typical Sanders store in the late 1940s or early 1950s. The top shelf in the display case includes a variety of pies. Pie staples included coconut custard, apple, cherry, lemon chiffon, mince, and chocolate nut. Ice-cream toppings and ice cream are on display behind the counter. Sanders bread is stacked atop the counter.

CAKE CUSTOMER. A customer purchases a cake in this photograph of a typical Sanders baked goods display case. Sanders bread is stacked neatly on the counter and on a shelf behind the display case.

SANDERS ICE CREAM. Sanders began mass-producing its popular ice-cream flavors for customers to purchase at grocery stores after the opening of the Highland Park facility. It was a logical progression for the company that had invented the refrigerator ice tray package, the beginning of retail, take-home packaged ice cream. The half-gallon-sized package shown in the picture proved to be the most popular.

ICE CREAM SUNDAE. Just when Sanders introduced the ice-cream sundae, and its famous toppings, in its stores is unknown. Ice-cream sodas were part of the menu as early as that very first summer of business. Sanders is credited with encouraging the popularity of the concoction as well as developing a successful retail business around the ice-cream soda. The sundae was a natural progression in the company's confections.

BOTTLED TOPPINGS. In the late 1950s, Sanders's famous ice-cream toppings were bottled in mason-style jars, as this promotional picture shows. Four flavors were bottled for retail sale: milk chocolate fudge, Swiss chocolate fudge, bittersweet chocolate fudge, and caramel butterscotch.

Canned Fudge Topping. This promotional photograph shows Sanders Milk Chocolate Fudge Topping available in cans. With its pure chocolate base and slightly caramelized flavor, the milk chocolate fudge topping is by far the favorite Sanders topping in the Midwest.

More Toppings. These bottled ice-cream toppings more closely resemble the bottled toppings available today in supermarkets, Sanders stores, and other retail outlets. Bittersweet boasts the strongest chocolate flavor; it has more chocolate liquor and less cream and sugar. In taste, the Swiss topping falls in between the bittersweet and milk chocolate fudge toppings.

THE PACKAGE DEAL. This Sanders promotional picture highlights the ingredients in the famous hot fudge cream puff: milk chocolate dessert topping, vanilla ice cream, and cream puffs. Although this photograph shows nuts on the hot fudge cream puff, Sanders stopped adding nuts to the dessert in the 1970s.

HOT FUDGE CREAM PUFF. The origins of the hot fudge cream puff, one of Sanders's most beloved desserts, is unknown. It is believed the concoction appeared on Sanders menus in the second decade of the 20th century, but just who thought to stuff a cream puff with ice cream and top it with Sanders unusual hot fudge also is unknown. In any case, the treat has been a staple ever since.

HOLIDAY PROMOTION. Chocolate Santas, still a Sanders favorite, add a festive touch to this holiday assortment of Sanders standards—honeycomb chips, the nibblers assortment, and butterscotch caramel topping.

SANDERS STUFFED STOCKING. Sanders's stock of candies for the holidays went far beyond chocolates. This photograph shows a stocking overflowing with Sanders treats, including striped taffies (candy cane kisses and peppermint stick kisses) and hard candies made by hand. Rounding out the assortment were cherry and lime sour hard candies and jelly beans.

The nicest of gifts — a stocking overflowing with brightly-colored hard candies, taffies and jelly beans. Each variety is bagged in see-through plastic and labeled for eye-catching, pegboard display. Sanders uses only fresh cream taffee, natural flavor hard candies, and gourmet jellies for the beans. Everything is Christmas-colored in white, green and red. Only Sanders has the candymaker skill to offer striped taffies and hard candies made by hand. Sanders wrapped candies in a cheerful fireside stocking, a customer-pleasing way to celebrate the holidays.

Candy Cane Kisses
7 oz. bag. Packed 12 bags per case
Shipping weight 6.4 lbs.

Peppermint Stick Kisses
7 oz. bag. Packed 12 bags per case
Shipping weight 6.4 lbs.

Cherry and Lime Sour Pusses
7 oz. bag. Packed 12 bags per case
Shipping weight 6.4 lbs.

Green Spearmint Dandies
7 oz. bag. Packed 12 bags per case
Shipping weight 6.4 lbs.

Fruit Brilliants (Cherry/Pineapple/Lime)
6.5 oz. bag. Packed 12 bags per case
Shipping weight 6 lbs.

Jelly Beans (Strawberry, Pineapple, Lime)
8 oz. bag. Packed 12 bags per case
Shipping weight 6.7 lbs.

CHRISTMAS HARD CANDY. Sanders's hard candies were holiday favorites and traditions for Detroiters at Christmas. This collection of hard candies included Kris Kringle sticks, sweetened almonds wrapped in red and green hard candy sticks; raspberry stufties, hard candy raspberries stuffed with Sanders's own raspberry puree; and peanut stufties, peanut-shaped hard candies filled with pure peanut butter.

Sanders hard candies are made by hand and taste the way you remember Christmas candy from childhood. Brilliant holiday colors and natural fruit flavors make these festive assortments a welcome holiday addition. Your customers will love the ribboned packages and removable gold price stickers, convenient for gift giving. All boxes are extra-wrapped to ensure freshness and come with see-through covers so buyers can choose just what they want.

Satin Stufties
Assorted luscious flavors wrapped in special satin-crunch coatings. A rainbow of pastel colors.
15.5 oz. box. Packed 6 boxes per case.
Shipping weight 6 lbs.

Hard Drops
Eight different, all solid, colorful flavors.
1 oz. box. Packed 6 boxes per case.
Shipping weight 6 lbs.

Kris Kringle Sticks
Sanders exclusive. Chopped sweetened almonds wrapped in holiday red and green hard candy sticks.
15 oz. box. Packed 6 boxes per case. Shipping weight 5 lbs.

Raspberry Stufties
Tender hard candy raspberries filled with Sanders own raspberry puree.
10.5 oz. box. Packed 6 boxes per case.
Shipping weight 5 lbs.

Peanut Stufties
Peanut-shaped hard candies filled with Sanders freshly made pure peanut butter.
10.5 oz. box. Packed 6 boxes per case.
Shipping weight 5 lbs.

Santa Hard Mix
The perfect stocking stuffer.
3.5 oz. box. Packed 24 boxes per case.
Shipping weight 6 lbs.

Christmas Hard Candy Tin
Just right for the lover of hard candy! A mixture of all of Sanders best in a Christmas tin.
16 oz. tin. Packed 16 tins per case.
Shipping weight 21 lbs.

VALENTINES ASSORTMENTS. Here is a collection of Sanders chocolates in heart-shaped boxes.

More Valentines Candy. Another retail display of Sanders Valentines products is pictured here.

Store Display. As Sanders began mass-producing its products, everything from candies to cakes, its confections were available on grocery store and retail shelves.

FAVORITE ASSORTMENTS. Sanders's favorite assortments include Soft Centers, the Nibblers, Milk Pavilion, Woodward (named, of course, after Woodward Avenue, the thoroughfare that proved so crucial to Sanders's success), and the Boulevard.

Soft Centers
Delight your taste buds with fruit creams, coconut creams, pecan and other creamy centers coated in milk and dark chocolate and smooth pastels.
1 lb. box. Packed 9 boxes per case
Shipping weight 12 lbs. 52 pieces per box.
2 lb. box. Packed 6 boxes per case
Shipping weight 14.8 lbs. 64 pieces per box.

Woodward
Dark chocolate favorites, Brazils and nougats, butterscotch caramels, coconut supremes, peppermint patties, maple walnut creams - just a few of the exciting centers in this assortment
1 lb. box. Packed 9 boxes per case
Shipping weight 12 lbs. 52 pieces per box.
2 lb. box. Packed 6 boxes per case
Shipping weight 14.8 lbs. 64 pieces per box.

Milk Pavilion
Rich milk chocolate-covered favorites, including nut fudge, fruit creams, Spanish peanut patties, Brazils, peppermint and chewy pieces.
1 lb. box. Packed 9 boxes per case
Shipping weight 12 lbs. 52 pieces per box.

2 lb. box. Packed 6 boxes per case
Shipping weight 14.8 lbs. 64 pieces per box.

Boulevard
Tender caramel centers and Brazil nuts, lemon, coconut and maple walnut creams and many more in milk and dark chocolate coatings
1 lb. box. Packed 9 boxes per case
Shipping weight 12 lbs. 53 pieces per box.
2 lb. box. Packed 6 boxes per case
Shipping weight 14.8 lbs. 66 pieces per box.

Sample Assortment
This smaller box duplicates all the favorites from the Boulevard assortment, a tempting mix of milk and dark chocolates.
7.5 oz. box. Packed 12 boxes per case
Shipping weight 7.6 lbs. 15 pieces per box.

Nibblers Assortment
Same selection of milk chocolates as our favorite Milk Pavilion - just a smaller assortment to tease the palate and to make you want more.
7.5 oz. box. Packed 12 boxes per case
Shipping weight 7.6 lbs. 15 pieces per box.

NEW PACKAGING. Sanders's favorite boxed chocolates were given a new look in 2002, after the brand's purchase by Morley Brands LLC, owner of Sanders Candy and Morley Candy Makers. Many of the traditional boxed favorites remained, including Boulevard milk and dark assortment, soft center assortment, Meadow Milk, and Pavilion milk chocolates.

Seven

THE SUBURBS

HIGHLAND PARK. Sanders's first store outside Detroit was opened in 1930 in the enclave of Highland Park. The first suburban store was a sign of things to come. By 1939, Sanders boasted 21 stores in and around Detroit, including Dearborn, Royal Oak, and Grosse Pointe. Highland Park also would become the home of the company's headquarters and manufacturing operations.

A NEW HOME. The entrance to the company's new office and manufacturing facilities is located at 100 Oakman Boulevard, Highland Park. The company had spent more than a quarter-century at the Henry Street location before moving offices and production to the nine-acre Highland Park site in 1941. The plant produced everything under the Sanders brands, serving the company's growing roster of stores. The plant remained in production until 1995, when Country Home Bakers of Connecticut sold the facility to a warehousing company. The Sanders distinctive lettering remained on the building as a local landmark.

AERIAL VIEW. The 425,000-square-foot plant produced all of Sanders's products, everything from baked goods to ice cream and toppings. After purchasing Sanders in 1988, Country Home Bakers spent $5 million on substantial improvements to the aging plant, including new lines for donuts and dinner rolls, a spiral freezer, new freezer compressors, new boilers, and new windows and floors.

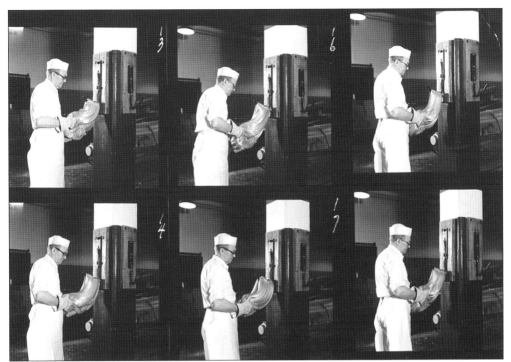

TAFFY HOOK. Sanders's famous honeycomb chips would have been nothing without the artistic talents of employees like Charlie Wass, who worked for Sanders for more than 40 years. Pulling taffy to create the multitude of combs was tricky business. The process involved pulling the hot taffy several times as it cooled and then rolling it on a table and turning it over and sealing it to create the honeycombs.

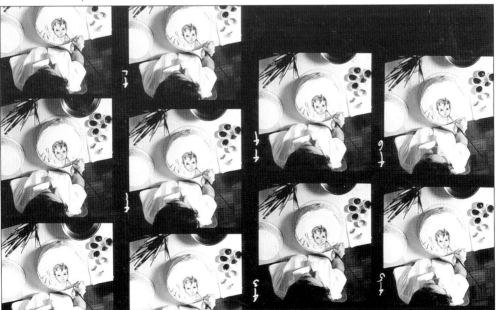

CAKE DECORATING. An unidentified employee puts the finishing touches on a specialty cake. The cake appears a to be a first birthday cake, a popular specialty order over the years.

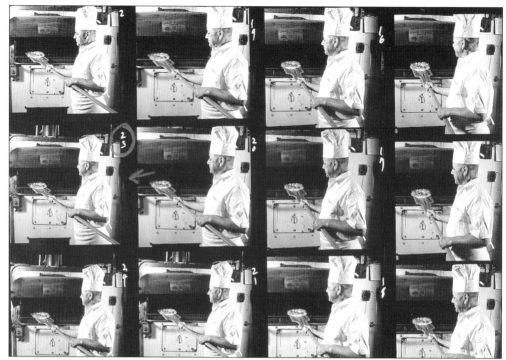

ALMOND RING. One of Sanders's most-loved pastries, the famous almond ring is shown in this photograph.

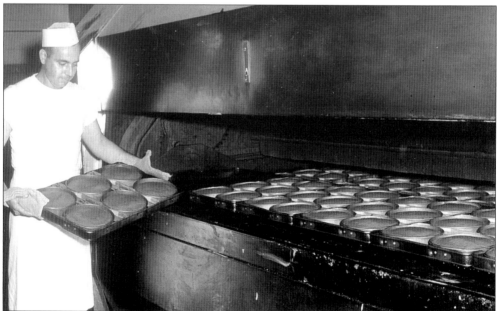

BAKING CAKES. A worker pulls a tray of chocolate cakes from the ovens at the Highland Park plant. Fred Sanders returned to his love of baking before his death in 1913. From the back of the Woodward Avenue store, the Sanders bakery always kept well within capacity. The stock was always fresh, and no perishable or yeast-baked goods were sold the second day. Surplus items were given to charitable institutions.

TURNOVERS. Dressed in white uniform dresses and green aprons, a group of women work an assembly line folding dough to create fruit-filled turnovers.

MORE TURNOVERS. The woman in the far right is removing prepared Danishes for baking.

SHEETER. An employee presses on dough being sent through a sheeter at the Highland Park plant.

CAKE LINE. A line of female employees puts the finishing touches on German chocolate cakes at the Highland Park plant.

CHOCOLATE CONVEYER. A conveyor belt of chocolates moves down the line at the Clinton Township plant.

PACKING GOODFELLOWS. Jack Sanders oversees the annual boxing of candies for the Old Newsboys' Goodfellow Fund of Detroit. Every Christmas, the former Detroit newspaper boys collected clothing, shoes, books, toys, and candy for needy children. The Goodfellow Fund initially bought the candy from Sanders, but during the Depression, Sanders began donating the confections, a tradition that lasted until the late 1960s or early 1970s.

BOULEVARD STORE. A counter clerk at the Woodward Avenue and Grand Boulevard store appears to be pulling a pastry from a window display for a customer at the counter. Anyone familiar with the streetscape would recognize the boulevard store from the retailers across Woodward Avenue. The Kresge Company stood next door to Sanders. This building still stands today.

LUNCHEON COUNTER. A counter clerk appears to be preparing something for a businessman at the luncheon counter. Long before there were fast-food restaurants, Sanders was a quick place to get something to eat. Businessmen on lunch could be in and out in 20 minutes. Note the paper-lined cone cups, a familiar sight at Sanders for decades.

DESSERT. A customer waits for his bill after eating a hot fudge sundae. Sundaes also were served in paper-lined cones.

YOUNG CUSTOMER. A boy sips an ice-cream soda at a Sanders store in the 1940s or 1950s. For many Detroit youngsters, going to Sanders for an ice-cream sundae was a treat for behaving during a grocery shopping excursion or a trip downtown.

WOMAN CUSTOMER. A counter clerk returns change to a customer who purchased boxed chocolates in an unidentified Sanders store in the late 1940s or 1950s.

SANDERS DELIVERY. Sanders delivered specialty and catering orders in a 1958 Ford emblazoned with the company's logo and then-colors brown, white, and peach.

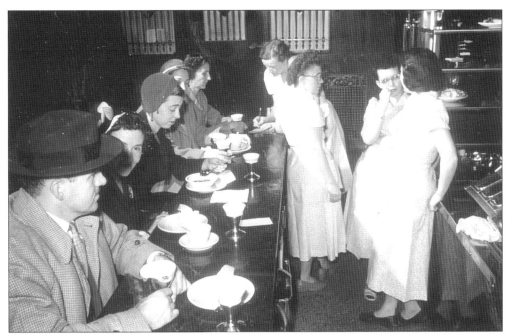

EMPLOYEE TRAINING. This photograph was used in a training program to demonstrate what counter clerks should not do. In this case, three of the four women are chatting instead of paying attention to customers. Sanders counter clerks underwent thorough training before working in the stores.

ANOTHER EXAMPLE. In another example of what not to do, the counter clerks are busy gabbing while a woman customer is trying to get their attention. Sanders counter clerks underwent rigorous training before serving customers. This photograph was made to show counter clerks what not to do. The length of their uniforms rose and fell according to changing styles.

WALK-IN FAVORITES. Sanders cupcakes and hermit cookies were favorites with walk-in customers, those who came in for a snack and did not stay for lunch or dinner. This photograph was taken at an unidentified store in the 1950s.

LUNCH COUNTER. This photograph of a lunch counter is believed to be one of Sanders's two Dearborn stores. One store was located at Michigan Avenue and Schaefer Road and the other in the Westborn Shopping Center, a high-volume store and one of the company's most profitable, at Michigan Avenue and Outer Drive. The narrow lower counter beneath the main counter served as a purse counter, a shelf where women could store their purses while they ate.

BRASS CHAIRS. The stools perched against the counter at this Sanders store are made of brass.

COFFEE CAKE LINE. Highland Park plant workers prepare long-form, fruit-filled coffee cakes for baking.

ROYAL OAK. This newspaper advertisement announces the opening of a second store in Royal Oak at the Northwood Shopping Center. The first Royal Oak store opened in 1935 in the Washington Square Building, becoming Sanders's 17th store. As Detroit spread northward along Woodward Avenue, creating new communities, Sanders followed. Like other locales, the Royal Oak store provided an array of Sanders products. According to a newspaper advertisement announcing its opening, the Royal Oak store stayed open until 11:45 p.m.

OAK PARK. The opening of each new store was advertised in the newspaper. Sanders was a regular advertiser in Detroit's daily newspapers, announcing the opening of new stores and new outlets for its products, as well as daily specials, baked good sales, and holiday products. One of its popular slogans in the early 1980s was "Sanders Makes It Better."

GROCERY STORES. Sanders's expansion into the suburbs included the opening of soda fountains in grocery stores, where customers could enjoy a hot fudge sundae or other ice-cream treats. This advertisement announced the opening of a Sanders department at the National Food Super Market in Mount Clemens. Initially Sander's supermarket activities were limited to the C. F. Smith stores, which eventually became National Food Super Market. By the late 1970s, Sanders was available in all major local chains, including Farmer Jack, Kroger, Great Scott, Chatham, and A&P.

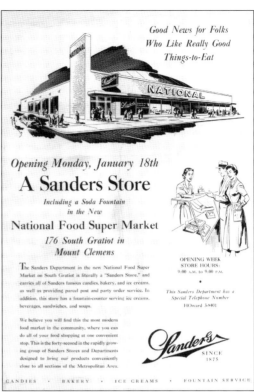

BIRMINGHAM STORE. This newspaper advertisement announces the opening of Sanders's first Birmingham store at 250 North Woodward Avenue. A second Sanders shop in Birmingham opened at 665 South Adams Road. By the 1970s, the Sanders's empire had nearly tripled in size, with more than 50 stores, stretching as far north as Utic.

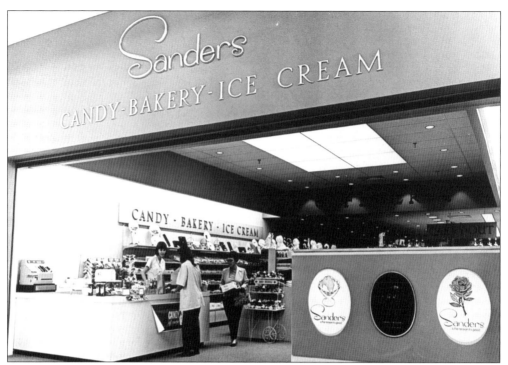

MALL STORE. Sanders opened two stores with this spacious, open design in the 1960s and 1970s. They featured open entrances, retail displays in the front of the store, and a cafeteria in the rear. Neither store was located in metropolitan Detroit. They were opened at malls in East Lansing, Michigan, and Toledo, Ohio.

INSIDE MALL STORE. Counter clerks are busy waiting on customers in the cafeteria of this mall store, probably the same one as photographed above.

SUBURBAN STORE. In another variation of a Sanders store in the suburbs, the counter is smaller and the store does not have the cafeteria-style lunch counters of other stores.

ANOTHER VIEW. This store also varies, with retail products stocked against the opposite wall. With a nod to the past, soda fountain tables and chairs are situated in the store center. Tiffany lamps hang from the ceiling. This is believed to be the basement of the Eastland Mall store, taken some time after a remodeling in the 1970s. The basement previously offered cafeteria service.

SANDERS BOWLING LEAGUE. Sanders bowling leagues started before World War II and continued until the 1970s. Bowlers included store clerks, managers, and plant and office workers. "We had tremendous bowling leagues," Jack Sanders recalled. "We were a close-knit company."

GROCERY STORE DISPLAYS. In the early 1950s, Sanders began selling its products, everything from bread and donuts to cakes and ice-cream toppings, in grocery stores. The program initially began with the National Food stores and evolved to include Kroger, Farmer Jack, and hundreds of independent grocers and drugstores. Ice-cream toppings and cakes are still available in some grocery stores in metropolitan Detroit.

BAKED GOODS. Another view of Sanders baked goods is seen here on display at a Detroit-area grocery store. One of Sanders's competitors, Awrey, has products on display in the background. At one time, the bakers sold their products in separate chains. In the mid-1960s, Sanders replaced Continental's Daffodil Bakers departments in Kroger stores in southeastern Michigan.

SANDERS DISPLAY. Sanders boxed cakes, breads, buns, assorted cookies, donuts, chocolates, and hard and soft candies are displayed here. Until the 1960s, supermarket retail operations had been limited to C. F. Smith and its successor stores, National Tea. By the mid-1960s, Sanders products were being sold in two strong local chains, Great Scott and Chatham. The National Tea stores in the Detroit market closed in 1966.

SUBURBAN STORE DISPLAY. By the 1960s, Sanders had introduced self-serve operations in many of its retail establishments. Customers could help themselves to an assortment of baked goods, ice-cream toppings and ice cream, and candies. At many of the shopping plaza stores, the menu was limited and the long soda fountain counter of yesteryear was no more.

CANDY DISPLAY. By the 1970s, Sanders had redesigned some of its boxed chocolates using a floral motif on white backgrounds. The covers of some boxed chocolates were printed with a series of chocolates. Standard boxed favorites, including the Meadow Milk and Pavilion, remained best sellers.

ROYAL OAK RELOCATION. Sanders opened a second store in Royal Oak at Thirteen Mile Road and Woodward Avenue in the old Northwood Shopping Center adjacent to William Beaumont Hospital. Like other suburban stores, this one was located in a small strip shopping center and probably was no more than 1,500 square feet.

INSIDE VIEW. This interior shot of the second Royal Oak store shows a small ice-cream freezer and retail displays.

TYPICAL MALL ENTRANCE. With the growth of malls in metropolitan Detroit in the late 1960s and 1970s, Sanders followed other retailers, opening stores in Oakland Mall, Eastland, Northland, and other locations. At its peak, the company had nearly 60 retail outlets in Detroit, southeastern Michigan, and Ohio.

LANSING STORE. In the 1960s to early 1970s, Sanders opened two stores in Lansing. One was located in the Frandor Shopping Center, a typical suburban strip mall near the Michigan State University campus in East Lansing. This is an exterior shot of the shopping center store being readied for business.

LANSING CUSTOMERS. The Lansing store differed from the suburban Detroit stores. Cushioned chairs and a cushioned bench against the brick facade were unusual.

PRESS CONFERENCE. Jack Sanders (third from the right), great-grandson of founder Fred Sanders and president of the Fred Sanders Company, answers questions during a press preview luncheon at the Sanders new Lansing Mall store, one of two that officially opened in the fall in the Michigan capital.

LANSING MALL. This Sanders store in Lansing was the first free-standing store the venerable company built. The store offered cafeteria service with a spacious dining area. Its line of candy, ice cream, and baked goods also were available at the store.

DELIVERY TRUCK. This undated photograph shows a Sanders delivery truck parked outside the company's Highland Park plant. By the late 1970s, Sanders had dozens of stores in metropolitan Detroit and supplied products to nearly 400 units, including the region's major grocery stores—Farmer Jack, Great Scott, Chatham, and A&P—and independent retail operations.

TROY SANDERS. The Troy Sanders Ice Cream Parlor opened at Rochester Road and Long Lake Road in the 1970s. The store was similar to those in other shopping centers, about 1,500 square feet and adorned in variations of yellow and green. The store stocked all the Sanders confections and had a limited menu. The store closed in the mid-1990s.

INSIDE TROY. This is a far cry from the heyday of Sanders's downtown stores, when customers would line two and three deep for a stool. In a nod to the old days, the Troy store featured soda fountain–style tables and chairs. Ice-cream sundaes and hot fudge cream puffs were staples.

ANOTHER VIEW. The Troy location was typical of strip mall stores. The walls and counters were green and yellow. In a nod to the forerunners, Tiffany lamps hung from the ceiling and soda fountain tables with marble tops and cast-iron stands were common. By the late 1980s, about 30 of the company's stores resembled the Troy shop, which closed in the mid-1990s.

ROSEVILLE STORE. Sanders's suburban stores improved in appearance as shopping centers evolved over the years. This Sanders store was located at Ten Mile Road and Gratiot Avenue.

SOUTHFIELD STORE. The Sanders at Twelve Mile Road and Evergreen Road was one of the few suburban shops to have its own oven to bake various Sanders confections, including pies, cookies, cupcakes, breads, and dinner rolls. Employees also iced cupcakes and donuts.

OAKLAND MALL. Here is a view of the Sanders store from inside the Oakland Mall at Fourteen Mile Road and John R in Troy.

INSIDE OAKLAND MALL. This is an interior view of the Oakland Mall store.

FARMINGTON HILLS. The Farmington Hills store was located at Twelve Mile Road and Farmington Road in the former Kendallwood shopping center. Although the store was small, it was extremely profitable. It had a 10-stool counter and a few tables. During the holidays, tables were turned into display settings to make room for customers.

INSIDE FARMINGTON. With a long counter, the Farmington store was decorated in the familiar yellow and green colors of other suburban stores. The store remained in business for more than 30 years, opening when the shopping center was first built. The counter and stools would disappear in stores in the outlying suburbs.

EASTLAND MALL. This Sanders kiosk is located in the renovated mall's Market East Food Court at the Eastland Shopping Center. Sanders also maintained a two-level retail store in the mall, with a basement cafeteria. That store remained open even with the kiosk. At Christmas, a second kiosk was opened in the mall to serve additional shoppers.

CLOSER VIEW. A close-up of the Sanders kiosk is seen here. The kiosk was the company's first step in the development of new retail marketing concepts. This kiosk, however, was one of the first Sanders operations to be closed when Country Home assumed ownership in 1986.

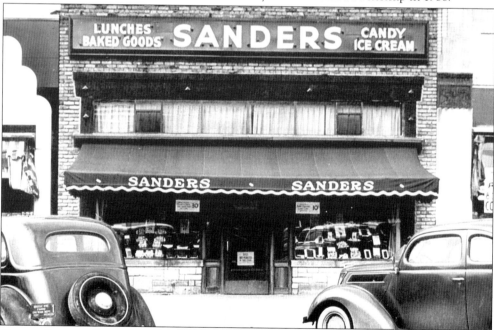

GROSSE POINTE. Opened in 1934, the Grosse Pointe store was a staple on Kercheval until the mid-1990s. With its marble counter, terra-cotta floor, and dark wood, the 3,600-square-foot store was a local institution and was honored with a plaque from the Grosse Pointe Historical Society. Residents rallied to save the store from closing in the early 1990s, winning only a short reprieve until Sanders stores completely disappeared.

BLOOMFIELD HILLS. Located at Telegraph Road and Square Lake Road, the Bloomfield Hills store was busy with eat-in diners and carry-out customers. The store contained a horseshoe-shaped fountain with 18 seats. The store was remodeled in the early 1980s and closed when the company went into its third bankruptcy.

INSIDE BLOOMFIELD HILLS. The remodeled store featured black-and-white checkered tile floors, pink trim above the back counter work space, pink and black bentwood chairs, and a self-serve ice-cream freezer in the rear.

WEST BLOOMFIELD. This photograph gives a peak into the West Bloomfield Store at Maple and Telegraph Roads before its remodeling in the 1980s.

ICE-CREAM COUNTER. The emphasis at this Sanders store was on ice cream. Unlike the early Sanders stores, the decor was simple. The white walls contained the menu board and a couple of posters advertising Sanders's hot fudge cream puff.

REMODELED STORE. In its first remodeling, the West Bloomfield store resembled others with pink and mauve colors. The West Bloomfield store featured a long counter with stools, just like in the old days.

WEST BLOOMFIELD. Seen here is an artist's rendering of the remodeled West Bloomfield Township Store. The store opened in West Bloomfield in the 1970s. The remodeling was part of the company's effort to revitalize its retail operations. When completed, the store varied slightly from this rendering.

WEST BLOOMFIELD. Like some of Sanders's other suburban stores, the West Bloomfield shop underwent a major renovation in the 1980s. This photograph of the store's interior shows the newly introduced lines of molded chocolates and truffles in the bulk candy cases.

C'EST SI BON. In the 1980s, Sanders purchased the C'est Si Bon product line to enhance its own offerings. This retail outlet opened in the Penobscot Building on Michigan Avenue in downtown Detroit, one of two downtown locales. Some of the products were also sold in Sanders stores, but the new products never caught on; Sanders customers preferred their own brands.

INSIDE ENTRANCE. This is a photograph of the interior entrance to the C'est Si Bon store on Michigan Avenue.

BAKERY CASE. After acquiring the C'est Si Bon line in the early 1980s, some new stores such as the Bloomfield shop carried a full line of the baked goods. The display contains an array of freshly baked croissants, Danishes, brownies, and European-style cakes.

FORD BUILDING. Long a staple in downtown Detroit, the Sanders location in the Ford Building was popular with throngs of workers in the nearby office towers. The cafeteria seated about 50 people, and the store did a lot of carry-out business. The store closed in the 1990s. A new retail store there still sells Sanders products.

Eight

TODAY AND TOMORROW

A 21st-CENTURY SANDERS. Tapping into Detroit's lingering fondness for Sanders, Morley opened a Sanders Candy and Dessert Shop at the Livonia Mall in September 2004. The store was an instant success. Running a retail store was nothing new for Morley; the company had three retail stores of its own, featuring Morley candies.

INTERIOR VIEW. Sanders Candy displayed framed photographs of founder Fred Sanders and other nostalgic photographs on the back wall and created a small counter where customers could eat their ice-cream sundaes or hot fudge cream puffs.

CANDY DISPLAY. As Morley's worked to bring back favorite Sanders products, such as the colonial buttercream and caramel cakes, they became available at the Livonia store. Sanders's variety of boxed chocolates, pictured here, as well as ice-cream toppings were big sellers.

SANDERS NEW HOME. Morley Brands LLC, another Detroit-area institution, bought the Sanders brand in 2002. The company had already been making some Sanders products for Country Home Bakers of Connecticut, the previous owners of the beloved brand. Morley's had been making Sanders chocolates and candy since 1994, perfecting original formulas and recipes. With brand ownership, the company began distributing and expanding the Sanders product line in metropolitan Detroit and elsewhere.

NEW GROSSE POINTE. After a short absence, Sanders returned to Kercheval in Grosse Pointe in November 2005. As officials worked to open the store, Grosse Pointers insisted on a having soda fountain in the new shop. The store has exceeded all expectations, and the company plans to remodel the Livonia store to add a soda fountain in the summer of 2006.

125

BEHIND THE COUNTER. Customers can also order a piece of their favorite Sanders cake. On this particular day, the devil's food butter cream, colonial buttercream, and caramel cakes are available.

SODA FOUNTAIN. Customers enjoy ice-cream cones and other treats at the new Grosse Pointe store, which serves a select menu of ice-cream favorites, including sundaes, milk shakes, and hot fudge cream puffs, as well as pop, coffee, and water.

MORE CANDY. With the opening of the Grosse Pointe store, a larger variety of Sanders candies and Morley candies are available in the store. The success of the Livonia and Grosse Pointe stores have inspired Morley Brand LLC to consider opening other stores in the metropolitan Detroit area.

ACROSS AMERICA, PEOPLE ARE DISCOVERING
SOMETHING WONDERFUL. THEIR HERITAGE.

Arcadia Publishing is the leading local history publisher in the United States. With more than 3,000 titles in print and hundreds of new titles released every year, Arcadia has extensive specialized experience chronicling the history of communities and celebrating America's hidden stories, bringing to life the people, places, and events from the past. To discover the history of other communities across the nation, please visit:

www.arcadiapublishing.com

Customized search tools allow you to find regional history books about the town where you grew up, the cities where your friends and family live, the town where your parents met, or even that retirement spot you've been dreaming about.